TURNING KIDS INTO CEO'S

A Complete Guide to Kids Business Ideas and How Kids Can Be an Entrepreneur

Turning Kids Into CEO's

Disclaimer

Copyright © 2020 by Arian Tucker.
All rights reserved.
No part of this book may be reproduced, scanned, or distributed in any manner whatsoever without written permission from the author except in the case of brief quotation embodied in critical articles and reviews.

First Printing: June 2020
ISBN: 978-0-578-70692-4
I'Jale Publishing Co LLC
www.ijalepublishing.com

TABLE OF CONTENTS

Turning Kids into CEO's 1
Table of Contents 3
Kids business and how to start it 1
Ways to Help Your Child Start a Business 11
Teach Your Kids About Entrepreneurship 18
Businesses You Can Start With Your Kids 23
Conclusions 28

KIDS BUSINESS AND HOW TO START IT

If you love to challenge yourself, go into business! Make an item or administration that you're energetic about and accumulate the materials and cash you need. Think of attainable business objectives and round out the best possible administrative work to make your business lawful. With training, you'll increase significant experience and certainty.

Building up a Business Plan

Record a rundown of things you're energetic about. If you don't, as of now, have a business as a top priority, conceptualize a few ideas. Make a rundown of the things you're genuinely intrigued by. These don't have to be businesses, yet just things you sincerely appreciate. For instance, you may understand music, building games, or playing games. If you happen to consider business ideas as well, that is extraordinary! For example, you may realize that you need to make armbands and sell them at a local event. Or on the other hand, you may simply record that you appreciate bands, playing the piano, or drawing.

Think of an item or administration to sell. Take a look at the rundown of things you appreciate and consider things you could make or do dependent on those things. This will be your business thoughts. For instance, in the case that you love kids, start keeping an eye on them. In the case that you appreciate drawing, make canvases or outlines to sell at nearby art fairs. You could transform a talent for PCs into work structuring applications. When you've chosen an item or administration, consider if you're most keen on bringing in cash with the business or whether you'd be more joyful treating it as an interest.

Assemble the materials and preparing you'll require. Make a rundown of all the hardware you'll require and request that a grown-up assist you with getting them. It's likewise critical to get preparing that is fundamental for the activity you need to do. For instance, in the case that you need to begin a Daycare, you should likely take caregiver and childcare classes.

You might have the option to get some less dense materials all alone if you have a minimal expenditure to work with. For instance, if you need to make armbands, you can begin by getting a few globules and gems wire at an art store. On the off chance that you need bigger gear, for example, a grass cutter, talk with a grown-up about obtaining or leasing the machine. Maintain your business face to face if you like working legitimately with clients. If you decide to sell your item or market your administrations face to face, discover an area, for example, area of the city. See whether there are any charges you have to pay to sell your things. To advertise administrations, think about going way to storefronts and leaving flyers.

For instance, sell natively constructed candles at your city week after week popup shops. To promote your finishing business, you may leave entryway draping flyers in your neighborhood.

Make an online social media and website to assist individuals with finding your business. Regardless of whether you're selling assistance, it's a smart thought to have a site so individuals can get in touch with you, read surveys, and see what administrations you offer. Set up other internet based life accounts so you can show photos of your work. Contingent upon how older you will be, you may require your folks' assistance to set up and run your online records. For instance, on the chance that you prepared a cake for somebody's birthday celebration, inquire as to whether you can share a photograph of the cake at the gathering.

Consider motivating forces you can offer clients. For instance, provide a slight markdown on the off chance that they pursue a regular help rather than a one-time administration. You can likewise arrive at clients everywhere throughout the world by running in any event part of your business on the web!

Make a financial plan and search for speculators. Cause a rundown of the considerable number of provisions you'll need to purchase, just as things that will cost cash once the business is going, for example, publicizing. Inspect how much money you have access to begin your business and how you will spend it. On the chance that you need cash to start the business, ask your folks or family on the off chance that they'd prefer to be financial specialists.

For instance, take a separated rundown of your business expenses to your folks and reveal precisely how much cash you have to fire up. Offer to utilize your very own portion cash or give them power over certain business angles, for example, showcasing. For instance, in case you're running an art stall, list the expense for leasing the space, the expense of tables or a tent, and the expenses for your materials.

Set practical objectives for your business. While it's a smart thought to have a couple of budgetary goals, for example, bringing in cash following a month or two, remember that there are different approaches to prevail in business. Give yourself reasonable goals, for example,

Building a client base

- Selling your item or administration in another setting or zone
- Getting new financial specialists
- Getting great audits from clients
- Setting up a Legal Business

Make a name for your business. Pick something that will make you stand apart from similar companies and utilize the name when you're enlisting the business with your city. For instance, unlike primarily using your name with your item, same to Beth's Beads, make an infectious name, as Bedazzled Bracelets.

Run an online quest for the business name so you can check whether somebody has that business name in your general vicinity. On the chance that somebody has that name, at that point, you can make another name that accommodates your business. If you need, create an eye-getting logo with your business name. Incorporate a trademark or adage to make it considerably increasingly essential.

Get a neighborhood license and pay any necessary changes. Request that your folks assist you with getting a business license. You'll need to go to the city corridor or utilize the region's administration site to get to the application structures. Likewise, you may need to pay an expense (which is as a rule around $50 in the U.S.), yet you'll be legitimately permitted to work your own business!

In case you're uncertain of what's required to set up a lawful business, contact a neighborhood private company affiliation and request direction. Check neighborhood public venues or do an online quest for secret venture relationship in your city.

Cover charges if you make more than $400 in a year. Monitor your pay and costs for the year. On the off chance that you just have a couple of charges, record them in a note pad. For progressively complex costs, use PC programming to log them. On the off chance that you earned more than $400, you'll need to make good on independent work charge. In any case, your folks will have the option to guarantee you like an award for their assessment purposes. However, you'll need to pay burdens on your business. For instance, on the off chance that you made $825 and burned through $200, you'd need to pay charges since you earned $625. You might need to put aside 10 to 15% of your salary, so you're set up to pay any duties you may owe.

Assessment laws change, starting with one spot then onto the next. On the off chance that you live outside the U.S., look at your neighborhood laws to discover on the off chance that you have to pay burdens on your business.

Disseminate flyers or utilize web-based social networking to advertise your business. Make or print signs and flyers that you can leave in shops, public venues, supermarkets, or schools. Utilize online networking to let clients pursue pamphlets, send coupons, or help them to remember up and coming deals occasions. Request that your clients leave surveys online to help spread the news about your business.

Reexamine your objectives in case you're battling. It's anything but difficult to be disappointed in the beginning periods of beginning a business, yet recall that your business needs time to develop! Develop a sharp item or administration and spotlight on dealing with your clients. On the off chance that you incline that you're prepared to surrender, come back to your objectives and think about changing your cutoff times or desires.

For instance, on the chance that you haven't had the option to turn a benefit following fourteen days, give yourself additional time, or set an objective of getting two new clients. On the off chance that you verged on meeting a budgetary goal, take a stab at defining a couple of littler objectives that will assist you with accomplishing it.

WAYS TO HELP YOUR CHILD START A BUSINESS

Try not to need your child to spend the mid-year staring at the TV, playing computer games, or grumbling that there's nothing to do? A late spring business can be an excellent method to energize innovativeness and certainty.

These business adventures aren't generally about bringing in cash. If an additional salary is a need for the late spring, occupation is the more secure course. Yet, beginning a business gives a significant beneficial encounter to kids, in addition to it grows pragmatic aptitudes like association, cash the board, critical thinking, and correspondence.

If your growing business person shows enthusiasm for beginning a business this mid-year, here are a couple of tips to help make the experience a constructive one:

1. Pick a business. Let them seek after their energy.

Significantly, your child is enthusiastic about what the person is doing. You need them to appreciate the experience and not lose intrigue and be back on the love seat before the finish of June.

If your child doesn't have a particular business thought as a top priority, have them make a rundown of their preferred activities. On the off chance that they love creatures, they could begin a pet-strolling or pet-sitting business. Possibly they need to make candles and sell them on Etsy. They could hold an acting workshop for more youthful kids in the area, show music exercises, or plan a portable application.

It's alright to break new ground. Zappos author Tony Hsieh began a worm ranch at nine years old, to turn into "the main worm rancher on the planet." Resist the desire to make statements won't work or that nobody would pay for their thought. This procedure is a learning experience; the final product doesn't make a difference.

2. Set objectives and make an arrangement.

Have your child consider all the stray pieces expected to transform their thought into a reality. What sort of hardware, supplies, or preparation do they need? On the off chance that they'll be cutting yards, what do they need? A yard trimmer, gas for the garden cutter, and so forth. On the off chance that they'll be child sitting, would it be advisable for them to take a CPR or emergency treatment course heretofore?

They ought to record their objectives for the business, including money-related goals and whatever else they need to accomplish. It will be fun and instructive to return to these objectives in September.

3. Present the idea of cash the executives.

A mid-year business is an extraordinary method to

acquaint kids with fundamental cash the executive's abilities just as multiple points like ascertaining gross benefits and overseeing overhead. Young people can monitor salary and business costs. More youthful kids can work on including value aggregates and tallying change.

You may need to give your child cash to launch their business. Provided that this is true, have them order all their direct expenses, so they realize precisely what amount is required. You could offer to finance a specific sum, as long as they contribute their very own portion birthday cash or payment. You could even hold a speculator meeting where your child tries out their plan to you and frameworks their monetary needs.

4. Work on client assistance and relational abilities.

Being a successful communicator and a compassionate audience is a fundamental structure hinders for business. Help your child grow how to clarify their item/support concisely and comprehend their company's offer. Stress the significance of client support, and urge your child to tune in to and oblige uncommon solicitations when required.

5. Deal with the legitimate prerequisites.

Child business proprietors are dependent upon the same standards and legitimate necessities from grown-ups. You can see whether any neighborhood permitting or allows required by checking with your nearby city/district agent's office.

At times, you may need to make a formal organization structure, yet just in case you're worried that the business will take off or put your family's advantages in danger. For instance, our most established child cherishes structuring applications. If it appears that an application will be monetarily fruitful on iTunes, we'll choose to move it under our holding organization. What's more, if we didn't have a holding organization, we'd structure an LLC

(Limited Liability Company) for it. You can choose the extent of your child's business and your family's risk insurance needs.

6. Cover charges.

If your child's profit is more noteworthy than $400, they'll have to document their expense form. No doubt, they won't be in a situation to owe any annual assessment. However, they should make good on independent work charges. Assist them with planning for this early - maybe saving 15 percent of the profit for charge time. They'll report their business pay and costs on Form 1040 Schedule C, and an independent work charge is accounted for on Schedule SE. Also, if you're pondering - indeed, you can, in any case, announce your child award regardless of whether they record their arrival.

The major and important thing to recollect is that the procedure ought to be enjoyable. The business enterprise is a work of affection, not merely work. It's likewise about taking risks, committing errors, gaining from those missteps, and doing it once more. Keep those messages upfront all through the excursion.

TEACH YOUR KIDS ABOUT ENTREPRENEURSHIP

At the point when you have kids, you need to give them everything, and more significant than things, that frequently implies showing them the abilities they'll require for glad, sure, and adventurous life. The business enterprise gives the capabilities that individuals of each age should be competent in our ever-evolving world.

While kids will most likely be unable to get a handle on the top to bottom subtleties of each part of the business that we as grown-up business visionaries are liable for, they're significantly more astute and intuitive than we are frequently given them kudos for. Kids' aptitudes and character qualities can learn as meager business visionaries will assist them with flourishing their whole lives.

So in case, you're a parent, and you need to begin

showing your kids the essential exercises of enterprise, don't pause!

Here are three straightforward approaches to start at present.

1. Assemble a lemonade stand.

On May 3, groups of children from everywhere throughout the nation set up lemonade and took an interest in national Lemonade Day. This occasion began in Texas in 2007 to help show the critical fundamental exercises of business proprietorship to kids. Through a progression of 14 activities, kids figure out how to set up their stand, name, market, and the various nuts and bolts of business creation and possession.

With taking an interest in urban communities from all aspects of the nation, from citrus-filled Florida to the far extreme north in Alaska (where they defer their cooperation to June because of snow conditions), there is an approach to begin taking an interest in your neighborhood.

Even though Lemonade Day has gone for 2015, you don't need to be in Alaska to get in on the activity this year. You can set up your lemonade, remain with your kids, and bolster an admirable motivation in June by taking an interest in Alex's Lemonade Days. Set up a remain from June 12 to 14 to urge business and to help children's malignancy examine.

2. Get the Kid entrepreneur's control.

Now and again, the hardest piece of encouraging anything is sorting out and organizing the information to impart to your kids. That is the reason my fiancé Kenneth, and I composed a book and showing manual for instructing business enterprises to children.

At the point when we became guardians, we were shocked by the absence of assets accessible for showing our kids business enterprise. At the point when we were unable to discover what we needed, we chose to make it. We've collaborated with instructive associations, schools, and after-school programs over the U.S. and Canada to get the word out about how guardians and instructors can get their children and understudies began youthful with the groundbreaking occupants of business enterprise.

In case you're a parent, and you need to train your kids about the enterprising things you do each day. However, you don't have the foggiest idea of how to begin; the Kidpreneurs site is an incredible spot to begin.

3. Getaway.

Next time you're contemplating hitting up Disneyland or Six Flags for your late spring getaway, consider an excursion to KidZania. What's KidZania? A huge amusement park for children based exclusively around enterprise and business investigation. It might sound less energizing than a trip to the mystical realm from the outset notice, yet one glance at its site or any of its recordings, and you'll need to take the kids there.

With areas everywhere throughout the world, KidZania is devoted to training children about the energetic yet significant parts of the business and the grown-up world we live in. It's an inconceivably all around planned and executed thought that will have your kids playing while at the same time realizing the stuff to be a business person.

BUSINESSES YOU CAN START WITH YOUR KIDS

We live in a period where the innovative soul is acknowledged and lauded. Individuals are beginning businesses regularly, and kids ought not to be prohibited from that. Many business ideas let kids express their creative minds, marvels, and abilities. Here are seven ideas to help get you and your kids began.

1. Children's book writer

Perusing stories with kids is a great convention, so why not think of one? It very well may be founded on your child's life and the amusing things they do or say, or the book can be utilized as a chance to instruct a real existence exercise like sharing or regard. Get your child's contribution to how they might want to build up the story. Extra focus if your child draws the work of art for the book.

2. Mentoring

This is an extraordinary business, to begin with, more established kids. On the off chance that they exceed expectations at a specific subject, let others know. Guardians are continually searching for approaches to support their kids, and regularly that can mean finding a mentor. As the parent, you can assist your child with things like driving them to and from coaching areas or overseeing mentoring meetings in your home. Guardians can likewise help with promoting by taking flyers to work or by posting them around town.

3. Looking after children pet sitting

Looking after children, pet sitting shows kids' duty. In the advanced age, landing positions like this are straightforward. Sites like Care.com and Rover.com are incredible assets not just to post your child's keeping an eye on (Care.com) or pet-sitting administrations (Rover.com); however, they are additional places to secure positions.

4. Yard care

At the point when kids are out of school, occupations like grass care are an ideal path for them to spend their late spring. In addition to the fact that they make some additional cash, they learn significant abilities for the future, such as tender loving care, practicality, and regard for others' property.

5. PC fix

Let's be honest; a few kids are higher at working with PCs than others. Experiencing childhood in the digital age has permitted kids to live and inhale innovation, making them specialists in numerous regions. On the off chance that this seems like your child, assist them with transforming their ability into a business by making flyers, publicizing their administrations via web-based networking media stages, and getting the word out. You can give a firsthand tribute about the nature of their work on the off chance that your child has helped you with your PC.

6. Commercial center merchant

The creative mind permits kids to make artistry, gems, and different artworks that intrigue the impulses of potential clients. If your cooler is secured with work of art, take it to the web. Nowadays, there are many choices for selling high-quality products; Etsy is not, at this point, the main alternative. With numerous online commercial centers, you get great postings, can set your costs, and get network support from different vendors.

7. Cleaning administration

Set out to utilize long periods of errands and urge your kids to advertise their cleaning aptitudes to other people. Things like vacuuming, tidying, and washing dishes are everything your child can accomplish for neighbors or relatives. On the off chance that your kids are more seasoned, you can incorporate undertakings like cleaning washrooms and wiping floors. You can promote on network sheets on the web or at nearby places like markets and libraries.

CONCLUSIONS

These businesses can be begun with your child and can show them feasible aptitudes for what's to come. Urge your young business visionaries to attempt their best and look for progress with their new business. Regardless of whether it doesn't turn out as arranged, you can give them that misfortune is a piece of life, and that disappointment is a chance to retool a thought or a way to another opportunity. The work experience additionally looks extraordinary when it comes time to apply for school and grant openings.

www.ingramcontent.com/pod-product-compliance
Lightning Source LLC
Chambersburg PA
CBHW070520090426
42735CB00012B/2849